MW00386797

Log Cabins
Past & Present

Tina Skinner & Tommi Jamison

Schiffer Publishing Ltd

4880 Lower Valley Road, Atglen, Pa 19310

Dedication

To my mom, Jeanette Thore, who has inspired me and reminded me that it's OKAY to love what you do, and to find a blessing in every opportunity, down any path you may take...

Schiffer Books are available at special discounts for bulk purchases for sales promotions or premiums. Special editions, including personalized covers, corporate imprints, and excerpts can be created in large quantities for special needs. For more information contact the publisher:

Published by Schiffer Publishing Ltd.
4880 Lower Valley Road
Atglen, PA 19310
Phone: (610) 593-1777; Fax: (610) 593-2002
E-mail: Info@schifferbooks.com

Please visit our web site catalog at www.schifferbooks.com

We are always looking for people to write books on new and related subjects. If you have an idea for a book, please contact us at the above address.

This book may be purchased from the publisher.
Include $5.00 for shipping.
Please try your bookstore first.
You may write for a free catalog.

In Europe, Schiffer books are distributed by:
Bushwood Books
6 Marksbury Ave.
Kew Gardens
Surrey TW9 4JF
England
Phone: 44 (0)208 392-8585
Fax: 44 (0)208 392-9876
E-mail: Info@bushwoodbooks.co.uk

Website: www.bushwoodbooks.co.uk
Free postage in the UK. Europe: air mail at cost.
Try your bookstore first.

Copyright © 2008 by Schiffer Publishing, Ltd. & Heathstone, Inc.

Library of Congress Control Number: 2008929599

All rights reserved. No part of this work may be reproduced or used in any form or by any means—graphic, electronic, or mechanical, including photocopying or information storage and retrieval systems—without written permission from the publisher.
The scanning, uploading and distribution of this book or any part thereof via the Internet or via any other means without the permission of the publisher is illegal and punishable by law. Please purchase only authorized editions and do not participate in or encourage the electronic piracy of copyrighted materials.
"Schiffer," "Schiffer Publishing Ltd. & Design," and the "Design of pen and ink well" are registered trademarks of Schiffer Publishing Ltd.

Designed by RoS
Type set in Niagra Engraved/NewBskvll BT

ISBN: 978-0-7643-3013-1

Printed in China

Acknowledgements

Many thanks go out to my family and friends, who have given up time with me to allow me to follow my dreams and work on this project. An extra special thank you to my children, Cody and Abela; they have been patient and understanding during the effort I have put forth on this endeavor. You are such blessings in my life.

I am also deeply grateful to all my teachers (especially Mrs. Sherry Sharp, who in the 6th grade showed me history can be fun and Mrs. Lynn Hatfield, who introduced the field of Interior Design to my world).

In acknowledgement, I would also like to give credit to Charles McRaven. He has influenced and educated many of us through his multiple publications, especially his book Building & Restoring the Hewn Log House.

Finally, much gratitude goes to Tina Skinner. We have worked on numerous projects together and she is a wonderful creative spirit, who has allowed this project to be such fun.

"We have to know where we've been to know where we're going…"

Contents

See how the floor joists stick through below the eave? That's how Hearthstone still builds homes today. These images were taken in the Cades Cove community in the Great Smokey Mountains of Tennessee, where a treasure trove of historic log cabins has been preserved. *Public Domain of Great Smokey Mountain National Park Library*

The Log Home Legacy
—Tommi Jamison

As settlers began to move in and explore the rural and undeveloped land of the United States, it became clear that they needed shelter. Shelter was a necessity: from the weather, from the rough terrain that surrounded the homesteads, and from native animals on the prowl for food. The elements that settlers faced were harsh and they were often near despair, which created a live or die attitude. The land was unsettled, unexplored, and uncivilized.

Around the seventeenth century, settlers from Sweden, Finland, and Germany were coming to the United States, and they brought their knowledge of log construction with them. Log construction became very popular because logs offered strength, sustainability, and offered flexibility for additions. The Homestead Act of 1862 promised 160 acres of free public land to anyone who would build a house, dig a well, build a fence, and farm at least ten acres—and do it for at least five years. With the passing of the Homestead Act, Americans took the knowledge from the European settlers and began to produce many log cabins.

The clearing of forest for fields produced large amounts of timber, in turn allowing for timbers to be cut on site. With the abundance of trees, it became very common to use timbers in many different forms. Timbers were used horizontally as logs for homes as well as for the exterior surfaces for barns, smokehouses, blacksmith shops, schoolhouses, and any other outbuildings that were needed. It wasn't long before settlers began to use timbers together vertically and horizontally to create large, open post-and-beam barns. The vast majority of the homes were built of logs hewn flat on the sides, with chinking (or mud) in between. Typically, the corners were joined with some variation of a dovetail-type notch. This basic technique was employed for technological reasons, which are still important and highly relevant today. The timbers were cut down flat (or hewn) on two sides, and cut down to a thickness of six to eight inches. To reduce warping and twisting, the heart of the timber would be in the center. On occasion, logs were split and both sections hewn, but this was uncommon.

Early on, there became a distinct separation and identification between log cabins and log homes. Log cabins were typically one-room structures, with no windows or chimneys. In most early cabins, there was only a hole in the roof to allow smoke to escape from the fires that were built for warmth and cooking. Cabins were often built on a plain dirt floor, with the logs sitting flat on the ground. This common practice created problems for what is known as the "sill" logs (the bottom logs that support the structure); because the sill logs laid directly on the ground, they were exposed to moisture and harsh elements that would damage them.

Round logs were notched in a Swedish cope style for corners. *Public Domain of Great Smokey Mountain National Park Library*

The vertical notches were hand-hewn with a foot adze on six-inch logs. *Public Domain of Great Smokey Mountain National Park Library*

Experience Counts

The knowledge to build better structures was gained by experience. A log "raising" became a neighborhood gathering, with many families coming together to build a cabin. At the end of the day, there would be a new cabin and a festive party for all who had a hand in the building process.

Log homes were identified as log structures that were hewn and stacked and also used stone and plaster in the chink area. The use of chimneys and glass windows were common in log homes. Both log cabins and log homes started as basic one-room structures, usually one story in height. The location of the fireplace on the gable end of the home was developed in the fifteenth century in England, but wasn't common in the United States until much later. This new design style allowed for less smoke in the upper areas of the home, which allowed for more living space to expand over the first floor. Timbers were used to create floor joists for this new living space, and it was very important that the timbers were cut from dry, seasoned wood. If green timbers were used for the floor joist, they could shrink and come loose from the walls during the process of the wood acclimating to the surroundings. These timbers were cut long enough to extend out over the logs until flush with the exterior of the logs in which the joists rest. The front and rear log that the joist bear on would have a mortise cut into them to ensure more stability and less movement of the joists.

This new living space is known as a loft, and most log manufacturers still use mortise joints or beam pockets in their loft designs today. Originally, the access to the loft was a vertical row of sturdy wooden pegs that were inserted into one of the walls. With the evolution of the loft area, the height of the homes increased 2-3 courses above the floor joist to accommodate easier maneuverability in the loft area. Very often, the children were shuffled to the loft area, while the parents were primarily located on the main level.

Expanding Homes

As families grew and expanded, so did the homes. It was very common for additional areas to be added to the original one-room structure as the family grew or as it was financially possible. Usually, the first expansion to be made would be a "lean-to." This would be a small space (often on the rear of the structure), and would usually run the length of the home. This space would have a roof that did not peak or have a gable, but would instead lean over onto the original structure. Today, this roof style is known as a shed roof. This new lean-to addition often became a kitchen.

On the rare occasion that finances permitted, a family would build a "two-pen" home. This design consists of two one-room structures that were joined with one roof. This design became known as the "dog-trot" style and is still commonly built today.

Very often, the new built-on areas would be constructed of materials other than logs, such as board-and-batten siding or other common building materials. Additions were built as the homeowners had time and/or resources permitted, and would have different surface finishes; they were built using whatever was available.

Not only were additional indoor living spaces added to the original structures, but porches were added as well. Porches were a necessity and had many uses, such as drying herbs, storing things (like washtubs), and hosting various activities made more pleasant by daylight and fresh air.

You can still find them: They sit atop the ridges, in the hollows, and on the stream banks of our nation. Like no planned or contrived monument could hope to, these 150- to 200-year-old log structures salute that almost indefinable and unique spirit that was, is, and always will be—America. A log home reflects the definitive American soul: the sweat, blood, self-reliance, ingenuity, pride, and unbreakable commitment to doing what must be done.

An Icon

Log cabins were claimed an American icon when General William Henry Harrison embraced them as a symbol of his presidential campaign in 1840. Shortly thereafter, a chain of presidents proudly acknowledged their birthplaces to log cabins including Polk, Buchanan, Lincoln, Johnson, and Grant. President Theodore Roosevelt glorified living in log structures after serving in the army near Medora, North Dakota. This site is now preserved as a historic location.

It would be hard to find a state that does not proudly preserve log cabins as roots of their history, whether occupied by famous persons or not. Many log cabins have been rebuilt to offer historical significance. Examples of this process are those cabins at Valley Forge, Pennsylvania, that sheltered General George Washington's army during the bitter winter of 1777. The Log Cabin Village in Fort Worth, Texas, is the result of a project by the Pioneer Texas Heritage Committee and members of the Tarrant County Historical Society who created a living history museum devoted to the preservation of Texas heritage. There are many cabins behind Southern plantation houses that have been restored and were originally inhabited by slaves.

Log cabins have provided more than safety and shelter throughout history; they have become a symbol of greatness and inspiration for the American Spirit.

A man holds up a measuring stick to illustrate the height of the timber, how big they were. It also shows how early builders used pieces of miscellaneous wood overlaid to fill in the cracks. *Public Domain of Great Smokey Mountain National Park Library*

Horizontal boards back the logs on the interior of a log home. The chinking has disintegrated over time. Shows the floor joists poking through beam pockets. *Public Domain of Great Smokey Mountain National Park Library*

Most cabins of the historical era were built in stages. There would be a main area, and then people would build a lean-to area (like that behind the chimney), after they had two or three kids and could afford the addition. This looks to be that style. *Public Domain of Great Smokey Mountain National Park Library*

The main area was built first with a loft up above, then the shed roof with the enclosure was built later. The two roofs are not connected. *Public Domain of Great Smokey Mountain National Park Library*

The chink space or gaps between the logs have been covered with regular dimensional lumber like batten. *Public Domain of Great Smokey Mountain National Park Library*

This image illustrates the common building tradition amongst early settlers—the process of building one area of the home and then adding on as they outgrew the space. *Public Domain of Great Smokey Mountain National Park Library*

Abraham Lincoln's Boyhood Home Site, 1811-1816
Between Hodgenville and Bardstown, Ky.
On U. S. 31 E.

CABIN IN WHICH PARENTS OF ABRAHAM LINCOLN WERE MARRIED
"IN OLD KENTUCKY"—K25

Historic postcards from the middle of the nineteenth century show Abraham Lincoln's boyhood home, and the cabin in which his parents were married. Lincoln's home was protected by a structure and made a national memorial.

Postcard of the Overfield Tavern in Troy, Ohio. This is a good example of beam pockets atop the first floor. Also, pieces of scrap lumber were used to fill in the chinking spaces. The wood aged dark, but today, a lot of homeowners are trying to recreate that look.

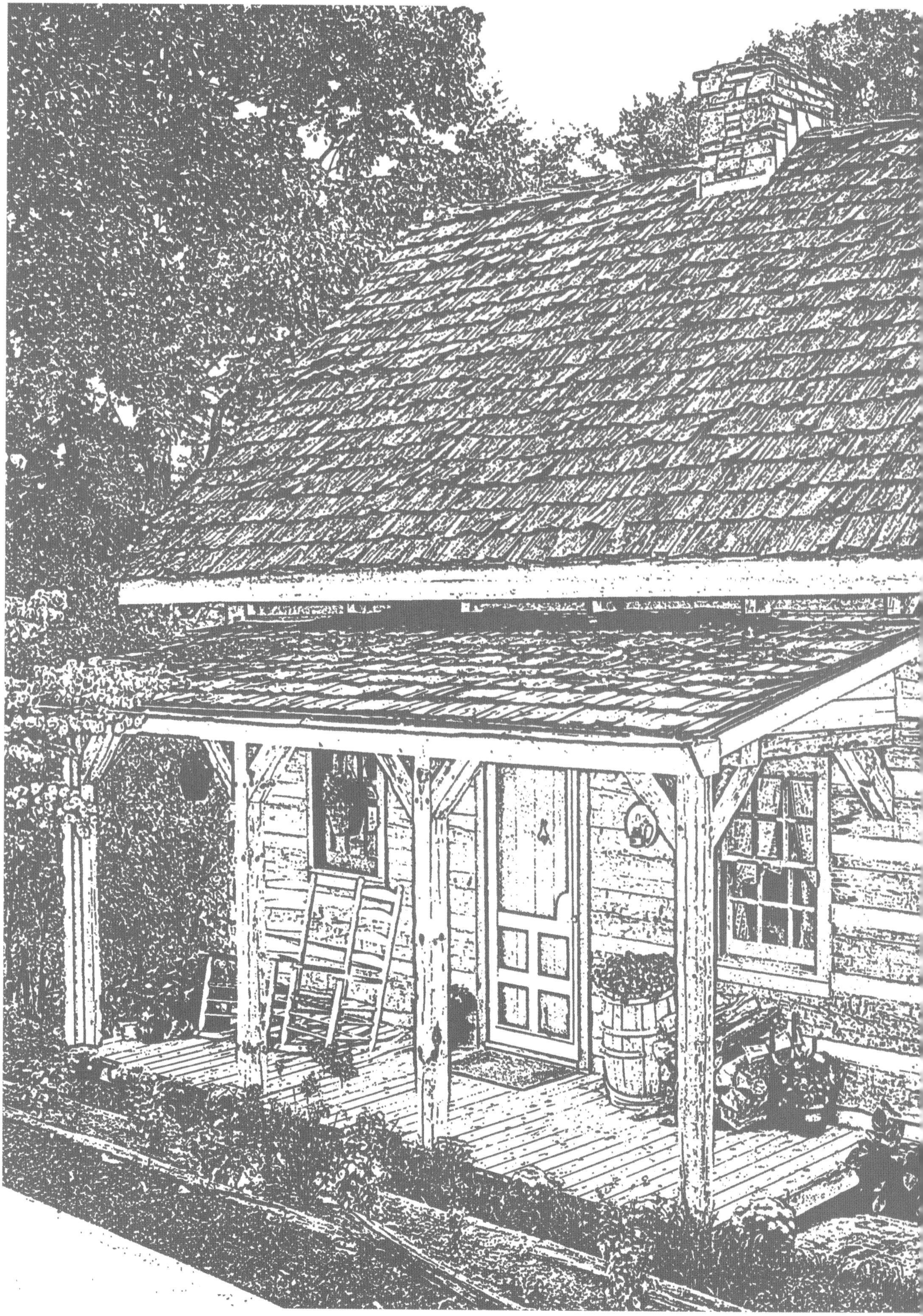

Log Homes Today
—Tommi Jamison

Log homes are a fixture of lasting architecture. They imply a historic, American, rugged way of life. Working long hours and enduring lots of hard work created a working homestead. It was a partnership between family members, with all members striving to make the homestead succeed.

Advantages and Appeal

The pioneers built their homes this way because of their outstanding technical advantages. We, at Hearthstone, believe in those technical advantages—as well as the tremendous aesthetic appeal. We build every home we create with that same spirit, tradition, and pride and believe that our log homes should authentically reproduce the look, charm, and aesthetics of our forefathers' homes. We then combine that basic philosophy with the finest in modern design, engineering, and technical details so that Hearthstone homes are enjoyed for many generations.

Nearly all of the permanent, long-lasting log homes of the past shared the common characteristics of logs hewn flat on the sides, joined at the corners with a dovetail-type notch, and chinked between the logs. While we have several different types of log homes, they all share these general characteristics. We offer logs that are naturally contoured on the top and bottom (at the chink joint), but hewn flat on the sides—as they were 200 years ago. They are a better-than-the-original reproduction of the look and feel of those 200-year-old homes.

All Hearthstone homes feature extensive technical specifications and techniques that promote centuries of use. We have many years and thousands of homes worth of experience and have led our industry in technical innovation and excellence for decades. The systems, engineering, and details built into each home—through the best of both handcrafting and CAD-CAM technology—are the key to the success of each project.

Hearthstone's Beginning

Hearthstone began thousands of homes ago in 1971, as a restorer of old log homes in the southern Appalachian Mountains. It wasn't long until there were more people who wanted those homes than there were old logs for restoration. So, we set about learning how to craft new homes—yet with the quiet strength of character of those original log and heavy timber dwellings. Though thoroughly designed and engineered to reflect our experience of thousands of homes and the best in modern technology and comfort, our log homes remain what they were at our modest, yet proud, beginning: faithful reproductions of those 150-200 year old, heart-stopping, hewn, and dovetailed homes that were the pride and labor of our ancestors. That passion still drives us today.

Over the many years, we have always focused on the art and trade of the Timberwright. Our company history, legacy, and culture make us different from others in this business. We have enough size to focus the appropriate resources on your project, yet we maintain that culture of commitment to the creativity and aesthetics of our Timberwright forefathers.

Early in the 1980s, our culture of handcrafting, heavy-timber construction, and historical reproduction led us to develop our timber frame homes. *Now most of our homes have elements of both log and timber frame construction.*

Options? Not a Problem...

Hearthstone is dedicated to making available to the public what we believe in: traditional, custom, American products of uncommon character. By providing products rich with a magical aura and a quiet dignity that makes eyes widen and imaginations spin, people have begun to realize that pride, respect, and craftsmanship still exist in the American marketplace. A really well-done log home is inspiring. You can sit and absorb one, and feel a special kinship with our forefathers of American history. There are few icons of that culture more compelling than a Hearthstone log home.

There are many manufacturers of log homes today, offering various styles of logs and many different versions of log homes. The options seem endless: round logs, square logs, irregular logs, logs with chinking, logs without chinking, and more. Each manufacturer has different styles and design practices, but most engineering details are similar. Hearthstone, Inc. uses a thru-bolt system, which creates a very strong, and lasting structure. This system uses heavy-gauge compression springs to tighten the structure to ensure minimal settling of the structure. The use of T-bar window jambs creates "floating" doors and windows and guarantees that any settling will not damage any of the components of the home.

Timbers are taken to Hearthstone's sawmill where they are de-barked and milled down into cants. The cants are then shipped down the road about thirty-five miles to our plant. The cants are unloaded and moved into "inventory." The timbers that will go into either the Vacuum-Kiln or into the Radio-Frequency kiln have "kiln" written on the timbers for easy locating. This will be removed during the manufacturing process.

Probes are inserted into the timbers as they are prepared for the Vacuum-Kiln for constant moisture measuring.

The Vacuum-Kiln must be full before a "charge" can be made; this kiln holds 25,000 board feet of lumber. Hearthstone, Inc. is the only company in the United States to offer vacuum-kiln drying of long-length timbers, up to forty feet in length. Drying in a vacuum means moisture exits timbers at a faster rate than a conventional kiln. The drying process within the vacuum chamber is highly complex, automated, and computerized. Moisture cables are inserted into several different timbers for monitoring. The drying process is monitored at Hearthstone, Inc. in Dandridge, TN and in Germany, by Brunner, the manufacturer of the kiln. For eastern white pine the drying time is approximately seven to ten days for a moisture content of 12-19 percent at the core. For oak species, the drying time is approximately thirty to forty-five days. For more information about the drying process go to www.heartdried.com.

The on-site control room of the Vacuum-Kiln in Dandridge, Tennessee.

Dreams Realized

Today, most Americans seem to have a long-lasting dream that has followed them from childhood into their adult life. They have always wanted and envisioned a log home; and usually have some idea of size, or a floor plan in mind. The current marketplace is filled with log homebuyers who are trying to escape from the hurried and rushed city life. These homes are being built in rural, uninhabited areas.

Timbers are loaded into the Radio-Frequency kiln. Typically, Oak is dried in this kiln because the radio-frequency kiln performs better with Oak than with other wood species. RF kiln holds approximately 3,500 board feet of timber. The drying times are approximately ninety-five hours for Eastern White Pine and seven to ten days for Oak.

Many log homes being built today offer more amenities than the cabins that were built by early settlers, but also present the feeling of a getaway. Some cabins today are built as vacation retreats or at a location where family and friends can gather and congregate. While others are planned as retirement living, they become enjoyed so much that the home soon turns into a full-time residence.

There are numerous ideas that clients bring to the table when designing their log homes. They want to capture a certain look, style, or design feature. Many clients have created a "scrap book" of ideas from miscellaneous sources (like the one you hold in your hands). The ideas come from pictures collected from magazines, books, home building/design centers, various travels, and firsthand experiences. They have envisioned what the final look will be, but often need help working out the structural engineering details to get the final appearance they envision.

Still other homeowners want to "recreate" an old, historic log home that they remember from years past; while some are going to extremes to create unusual and unique log homes. The desire to have an original-looking home that nobody can duplicate inspires homeowners' creativity. They are taking on the task of architect, designer, decorator, builder, carpenter, contractor, and laborer. They are putting a part of themselves into the home, so it is much more meaningful and important.

Often, families work together and build their log cabin as a "family project." When taking on so many responsibilities, these homes become more of a family treasure and keepsake. When so much is poured into creating a home, it is usually passed down from generation to generation, and becomes a gathering place to feel safe and for making lasting memories.

Timbers are fed to the K1 machine line for computerized processing. The timbers are lifted up to the machine that will drill the wire holes for the logs and create the dovetails and any additional notching, such as beam pockets or tenon joints.

Families Design!

Clients who build these log cabins take many design features into consideration. They may be planning for their senior years, or for the needs of aging parents, as well as visits by adult children or younger grandchildren.

Homes are being built with many modern conveniences, and create a luxury atmosphere. Most all homes today are built with at least one master suite on the main level (very often homes will have more than one master suite on the main level). Some designs feature one-level plans, while others use multi-level plans.

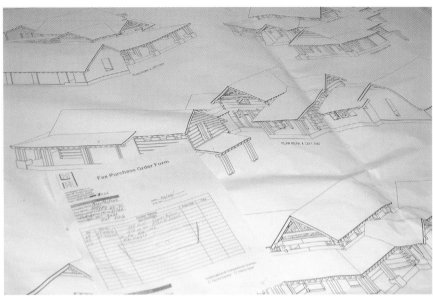

Clients are designing their homes to suit their lifestyles. They are thinking of family members—their likes and dislikes—to create a unique and one-of-a-kind home. For example, if a favorite pastime for a family is playing games, they create a comfortable space for playing, as well as storing, the games. This allows the home to feel well kept and tidy. Having a place for everything to be stored allows a more freeing lifestyle, a less stressful atmosphere.

If a family pastime for creating memories is cooking large holiday dinners together, then most likely, extra time and effort will go into the kitchen design. More often than not, the kitchen and living areas feature relaxed and open atmospheres. Expansive, open spaces allow multiple family members to work in the kitchen and prep areas together, and allow other guests to join in the conversations while not interrupting the workflow of the kitchen.

Other clients want to give their guests their own space. They are providing "bunk rooms" for the grandchildren and "suites" for guests. The bunk rooms often have multiple beds with fun design features; such as play-area lofts with unique ladders, swings hanging from the rafters, peep-hole windows, private/personal TV/ DVD areas, and reading nooks.

Log cabins today are more accommodating and luxurious than cabins of the past. Decades ago, cabins were built as a necessity for shelter, as protection from various elements. Today, cabins (whether large and expansive or small and cozy) are being designed as an extension of the diverse

A set of plans provides guidance for workers about the home that is currently being cut on the Hundegger machine. Each home ships with a package that contains "production prints," plans, and perspective drawings of the home, with each timber labeled. There are "exploded" views to help the building crews see which piece goes where. Each timber is individually labeled and the label corresponds to the "part number" listed on the drawings. For production plans, each piece is labeled on production prints AND in the machine file (that is supplied to the computer).

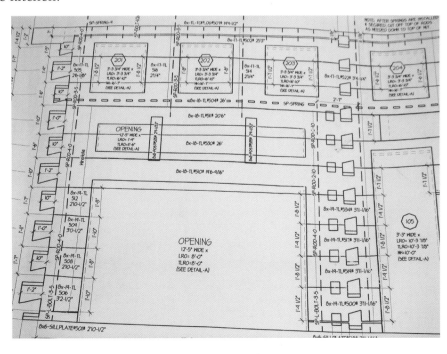

homeowners. Often, the homes feature luxurious master suites, with lounge and bath areas that allow a temporary escape from the surroundings (and sometimes reality). There are outdoor showers, saunas, hot tubs, beautiful gardens, and separate guest cabins. Every detail is well thought through.

An example of detail: A visit to a home we built just outside of Charleston, South Carolina, illustrated just how well homeowners are planning for their guests. Opening the closet doors in a guest bedroom to observe closet space, it was clear to see the homeowner had thought of every detail—including the handmade hangers in the closet. The property consisted of 1,600 acres, and branches had been gathered for the sole purpose of making clothes hangers. The branches were drilled and large "S" hooks were inserted for hanging on the closet rod. Small details such as these are sure to make guests feel as if everything has been considered to make their stay perfect.

There are endless stories from homeowners that have similar outcomes. Clients are pouring themselves into their cabins. Another cabin, which was built in Jonesborough, Tennessee, has other inspirations. The homeowner used walking sticks from numerous visits to "The Swag" as towel holders in their cabin bathrooms. ("The Swag Country Inn is an intimate hideaway that invites you to discover the wonders of nature just steps from your bedroom." The inn is located just thirty miles outside Asheville, North Carolina.) They also "recycled" wood from a local barn that was being torn down. The barn wood was old and abused. Vines had to be scraped from the boards and finish applied to all surfaces.

Putting so much love and passion into your cabin is a rewarding feeling. It can be compared to the early settlers and their homesteads. The success of early homesteads depended on the contribution of the entire family; today, clients are trying to get back to that place in time. They want to connect with their forefathers, they want the heart-stopping, jaw-dropping effect of a hand-crafted home.

They want an *extraordinary* home, and for that, they come to Hearthstone, Inc.

This image shows the finishing line where the timbers come off the K1 or K2 line after the wire/thru-bolt holes have been drilled, the dovetails have been cut, and the grooves for the spline/backer boards have been created (for the application of the chinking). At this point the timbers are "labeled" with the part number, corresponding to the number indicated on the drawings.

Each piece is individually labeled with a part number. This label contains coded information such as the customer name, wood species, size of timber, if the timber is hewn or planed, and log profile.

These floor joist show the mortise joint for the beam pocket. These timbers are to be used with bark still intact. They have been milled and cut and are ready to go to shipping for loading and delivery.

A mortise and tenon joint is used to lock two timbers together when wall lengths need to be longer than the standard forty-foot log. After pushing the timbers together, holes are drilled into the joint and wood pegs lock the joint together.

On occasion, smaller logs require adjustments with cutting notches, etc. because the logs must meet a minimum timber length to go through the machining process.

End pieces and scraps are collected daily and taken to a scrap pile. These scraps are given out free to the local community to use as firewood.

Log veneer is manufactured and kept in stock for use when the need arises.

Hewers use a foot adze to create the hand-hewn product.

On occasion, additional cutting/milling will need to be done by hand, as seen here.

A home is loaded onto flat-bed trailers. It will be covered and delivered to the building site.

Exteriors

Take a drive by homes that harbor ancestral aesthetics, mimicking in beautiful detail the hand-crafted appeal and early design principles of America's first homes. These homes are relatively new, however, and also embody the best technology available for comfort and efficiency. For anyone planning to build a traditional-style log home, this is a great opportunity to study a variety of authentic profiles and color schemes.

The studio of Bob Timberlake in Lexington, North Carolina, and guest house. Timberlake is known for his paintings and design work ranging in products from clothing to furniture and architectural products.

This guest house on the complex owned by artist Bob Timberlake, has been the inspiration for many of his paintings. It embodies the principles he has brought to log home design with the irregular logs, the wood cedar shake roof, and irregular log porch posts.

The Flag House is another structure designed by Bob Timberlake and indicative of his rural Americana ethic.

Ashville School is a private boarding school in Asheville, North Carolina. Two cabins donated by an alumnus serve as an outdoor learning center and a cabin for one of the teachers. The style of home was selected to fit into the mountainous surroundings.

The homeowners personalized this home by inserting coins and decorative rock and other souvenirs and treasures from their world travels. A casual observer would never know that this is just a log veneer; the chinking spaces are standard, and the dovetail corners lend authenticity. The chimney of river stone is capped with copper to match the copper downspouts. Typically, we erect the logs and the homeowner's builder will do the chinking. Load bearing blocks are inserted between the logs to transfer overhead loads to the foundation. Insulation is then placed between the logs and load bearing blocks. Spline board and spline gasket are then positioned into the spline groove. The chinking is then applied to the spline board.

Located in Pigeon Forge, Tennessee, this log home was created as a vacation home built with two master suites for the two couples that co-commissioned. The porch was put on when we constructed the house, so the porch rafters lay on the main roof rafters.

A good example of different materials being married in one building— a log home serving as the center, surrounded by shakes for the roofs, copper gutters and downspouts, and the stone extension.

The homeowner's goal was to build a home that resembled a style from the past, where it was built in stages, just like the original settlers used to do. So they did the major center wing in log with the chimney, and master bath wing in board and batten siding, another wing in log, and a separate garage attached via a covered breezeway. The central roof is the highest to represent the first structure that was built. The additional structures have a lower pitch and connect to the center roofline via valleys.

This homeowner wanted to use local materials to complement the logs. He used Pennsylvania stone from a quarry a couple miles from his home on the foundation and the office wing, as well as the chimney and fireplace. He accomplished recreation of the separate roofline for the main home and the shed porch roof. Doghouse gable dormers were created that left the main roof open in front of them for a different effect.

Here, a shed dormer is shown; a portion of the front porch is a screened-in porch so that the family could enjoy outdoor living. Board and batten siding was used on the gable ends.

A home in Townsend, Tennessee, using the Bob Timberlake® log profile, which is an uneven log that follows the natural contour of the timber. Irregular sizing creates an irregular chink space as well. The logs may be 14 inches high on one end, but go up to 24 inches at the other end of the log wall. This homeowner does not have a second floor. She wanted a cathedral ceiling throughout. To allow for additional light, she used clerestory windows on the front and rear of the home.

Bob Timberlake® logs extend up to the roof peak of the gable ends on this home. A clerestory window above the entryway admits light into the central cathedral area of the home. An iodized tin roof creates a contrast on the porch roofs. Rhododendron railing on the porch entryway adds a rustic feeling.

This guesthouse was built with logs from the Bob Timberlake® Log Home Collection. A rear lean-to addition mocks the additions that would have been made in earlier times and serves as the kitchen. A gable dog-house dormer in the front illuminates a small loft bedroom.

Two stories of full log make this home a standout. A single-story screened-in porch is very unique, as well.

Random stack hand-hewn Oak logs of 8, 10, and 12 inches in height create a rustic appearance for the Wyoming home. The logs were treated with an aging agent to create a weathered and worn appearance that flatters the rustic flat fieldstone on the central fireplace. Blue window framing creates contrast. A wrap-around porch is supported by a timber frame technique of posts with angle braces.

This home incorporates different finishes for the gable dormers to create contrast with the log walls. The standard porch roof bears on the main roof.

Naturally contoured Bob Timberlake® logs allow this cabin to sit comfortably at home within the tree line. The homeowner was trained as an architect and designed his own floor plan for this North Carolina home on a hillside overlooking a lake. A board and batten-sided lean-to houses the master bath. Guest quarters are upstairs. On the rear of the home, a large gable porch and screened-in porch extends from the main home toward the lake, with an outdoor fireplace and dining area.

Full logs for this two-story home, plus an attached single-story office off the master bedroom with a wrap-around porch and a timber-framed dining area wing. Out back, a brick wall creates a private courtyard with an outdoor fireplace and bar-b-q area. Steps off the brick patio lead down to a lake.

This small house is actually a three-story home, with a walkout basement that contains living areas. It's one-and-a-half stories in log, with regular siding for the gable ends. The owners wanted a historic profile, so they constructed a separate porch roof attached to the logs under the main roof, and cedar shakes for the roof.

A three-story Bob Timberlake® log home features a shed roof on the rear of the home allowing for additional head height on the third floor, as do the three gable dormers on the front. Decorative smaller windows tucked in the gable end offer a unique exchange of light for the third floor.

A large, two-story log home with a walk-out basement and a covered timber-frame carport. The over-sized fireplace is in keeping with the scale of the home.

This is a standard house plan offered by Hearthstone called the Greenbriar, with one-and-a-half-story log cabin including an open loft and living quarters on the main floor.

A lakeside cabin has logs that extend up to the roof peak, very simple and offers the minimum you need.

Built as a mountain cabin to escape the stress of city living, it offers an open living area on the first floor with an open sleeping loft above. A metal roof is extended by a porch overhang, overlooked by a single dormer. Typically, a porch roof is inset two feet on each side from the main roof to create interest in the surface plans.

A simple country cabin has an extensive screened-in porch and large over-sized fireplace characterizing this home. Inside is a cathedral space with no loft above.

A LaVeta, Colorado home marries log with adobe-style stucco. All one structure, the homeowners were going for the look of an ancestral home that expanded over time.

The original structure, a bed and breakfast, burnt down and the homeowners rebuilt this three-story log home to recreate the original historic structure. Now a private home, with walkout basement, a fireplace on either end of the structure, and covered porch areas on the front and rear of the home.

Unique horizontal windows flank the fireplace so that you can still have wall space for cabinetry or built-in furniture. The covered porch on the front of the house is handsomely framed in timbers and a crosshatched railing. A deck extends from the back for a woodland view.

This two-story log cabin has a screened-in porch on the basement level as well as the first main floor. The covered porch on the front is situated under a raised main roof with gable dormer on the top floor. The dry-stacked stone of the fireplace and the Bob Timberlake® log profile give the home its rustic appeal.

This lakeside home in Wisconsin is a full two-story log structure with an offset porch that ties into a one-story extension. Oversize windows are a modern improvement on the historic log cabin.

The main home is connected to the garage by a log breezeway. Both the breezeway and garage are finished with a log veneer to match the 6 x 14-inch log structure of the home, with 3-inch chink space (a Timberwright® log profile). The wrap-around porch creates extended living. Gable dormers on the second floor allow for additional space.

One and a half-story log home with an offset fireplace, cedar shakes for the roofs, a main roof that is raised above the porch and lean-to roofs to create a different slope for the separate roof planes.

This style home is a dog-trot floor plan, which means there are two wing sections accompanying a central section. This old design was used by early settlers who would build one wing for the family and one wing for an in-law suite, connected by one roof and an open area in between where the dogs would often lie. Here, a shed roof opens up a two-story cathedral ceiling in the back of the home, while a loft in the front houses a master suite.

Oversized gables above a full-length front porch give this home its unique profile, and creates lots of living space upstairs. The home was designed around treasured antique furnishings and other sentimental heirlooms. A large home, it includes a lot of unique roof-lines with over-sized gable dormers, spacious front porch, side bump outs, and a covered stoop.

A guest cottage at a nature resort was given a darker finish to integrate it with the forest scenery of Maryland.

This family project was initiated by a father who wanted to help his youngest son test his interest in architecture prior to his going off to college. The family did all of the finishing work themselves on a weekend retreat on a pond in Ashland, Ohio.

Entryways

$\mathbb{B}$esides enhancing the street profile of a home, an entryway is a visitor's first memorable impression. The construction and the furnishing of this first step is an important first sentence in a homeowner's personal introduction. Designed to create that initial impression, these entryways exemplify various ideals in approaching the log home. The ideals vary from grand to humble, all crafted lovingly to embody the owner's ideals.

Humble chairs, an old fashioned broom, and a careful canopy of grapevine provide a simple welcome.

A broad staircase beckons visitors forth
toward a warm brown front door.

Tapered stone pillars recall the Arts and Crafts Era, appropriate in a home where the owners worked to embellish the chinking with decorative stone and personal souvenirs. Character posts support the portico roof.

A gable porch adds awe to this log and stone hybrid home.

Natural cypress timbers were harvested from the property in which this home was built. The cypress posts frame an artful, one-of-a-kind entry door that was made on site by commissioned craftsmen.

Stone backs a recessed entryway, allowing visitors approaching the door to first admire the dovetail joinery of the log construction.

A bark veneer and wooden framework add character to this elegant entrance.

Front Porches

Porches have served many purposes over the centuries, from yesterday's shady spots where potatoes were peeled to today's impressive places where guests are greeted. The size of a front porch is generally based on an owner's intent to use it, or simply to show it off. In many neighborhoods, a front porch is an opportunity to keep a lookout and send a "shout out" to friendly neighbors passing by. In many cases, though, all that's needed is a sheltered stoop where groceries can be laid to rest while unlocking the door, or where a guest can escape the rain while waiting for a response to the doorbell.

A cypress tree seems to spring from the floorboards of this covered porch, as natural as the bent willow chair beyond.

Rockers furnish the quintessential log cabin porch.

Stacked wood and simple rockers add to the rustic appeal of this porch retreat.

Candelabras overhang a welcoming front porch and give the height
of the porch timbers proportion.

Furnishings keep a low profile, emphasizing the beauty of the logs that stacked to form the first story of this home.

Adirondack furnishings and garden accouterments set a country tone for this front entryway.

Character posts support a shed roof overhang and shelter a recessed opening.

Rustic furnishings add delight to a front porch and create a spot to enjoy conversation with visitors.

His and Hers chairs command a view of the entryway.

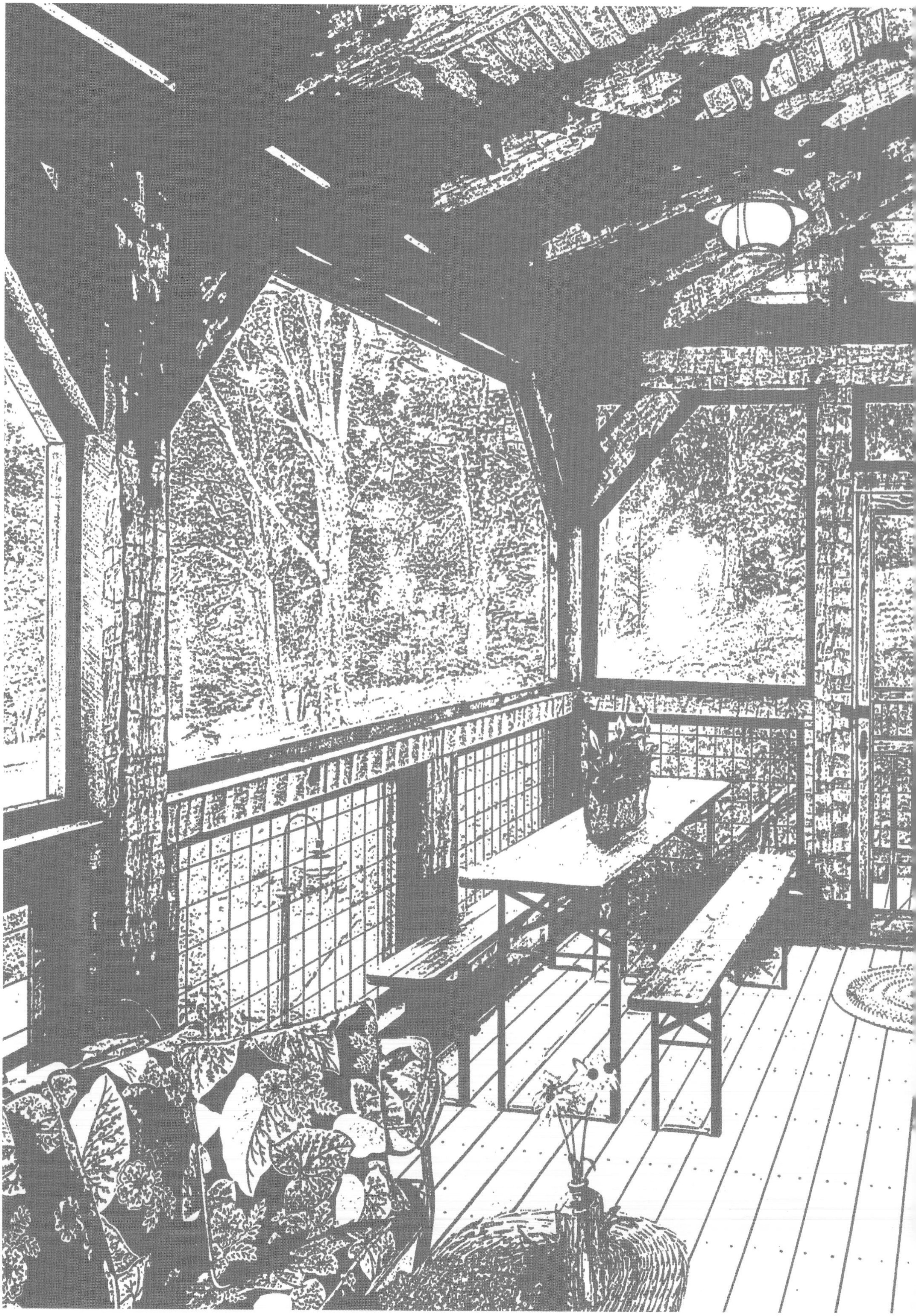

Back Porches

Whereas a front porch was designed to welcome visitors, a back porch is the place where family and friends can escape for privacy. A back porch is the perfect outdoor retreat, available for escape three seasons out of the year. Whether screened or open, the porch offers protection from sun and rain, while opening up the home to fresh air. A strategically-situated back porch can be an extension of living and dining spaces, or it may double as mudroom, providing a transition area from clean home to messy outdoor chores. The location and amenities of a back porch are an important consideration in planning a custom home.

An extensive back porch is dominated by a central fireplace, bringing an inside amenity to the outdoors. Chains extend from the gutters; to create downspouts into catch barrels that are used to distribute the rainwater, an old fashioned system that is becoming very popular again today.

Weather-aged tree trunks support a shed roof and add interest to this backyard and the brick patio beyond.

Padded rattan chairs make this back porch as comfortable as a sunroom, without the walls.

A finished floor on this extensive back porch provides a seamless transition from inside to out to a screened porch beyond.

A variety of seating is in the offering for visitors to this porch. Rhododendron adorns the open porch eave beyond.

A decorative tree ascends through a screened-in back porch.

A screen wall wraps a rambling back porch, complete with outdoor fireplace. The homeowners used screen under the floor decking to ensure bugs and insects won't invade this special dining area.

Wide floor decking, stone, and rough-hewn posts add to the ambiance of this screened porch.

A fireplace warms a screened porch, a favorite hangout for al fresco dining or catching up on a good book.

Foyers

A foyer or entry hall serves many purposes. For the family, it is the storage center for outerwear, and is usually outfitted with a mirror so that everyone can check that they are presentable before marching out into the world. A well-furnished foyer provides a place for keys and purses, storage for wet umbrellas, and racks for wet or muddy shoes. In many cases, these functions have been pre-empted by a garage entry into the home, or another form of family entrance, thus leaving the foyer pristine for its other function of greeting guests. For guests, the foyer provides a first impression of the home's interior, and a point where they are welcomed. From simple hallways to elaborate entrances, we've assembled a few ideas for welcoming others into your home.

Log outside is repeated inside, reinforcing the character of this country home.

An elevated stone platform forms the stage for an introduction within the timbered entrance of this home.

A sense of tradition mixed with humor welcome first-timers to this log cabin home.

Just beyond the threshold, a visitor is inside this casual home.

A cross-section slab of a tree is inset in this stone foyer for an awe-inspiring accent.

This stair rail was finished to match the hand-hewn posts, which greet guests in this uncluttered and simple entry.

Living Areas

njoy this opportunity to tour the great rooms, living rooms, family rooms, and dens of private log homes around the country. This private glimpse offers an opportunity to visualize how others have furnished their fantasy log homes, and how they relax and entertain in them. This section explores the places where everyone comes together, where memories are made. and the workday is forgotten.

Wood and faux stone team up, to re-create a "castle" inspired theme for this homeowner who studied at Oxford.

Colorful furnishings add punctuation to a room framed in log and fieldstone.

Furniture is arranged casually around the central brick hearth, overlooked by great log beams.

A gray finish creates a stately appearance for a sitting room, complete with a paneled fireplace and window moldings in antique tones of red.

This homeowner used two-tone logs to replicate the unstained and untreated log homes of the Early Appalachian Era.

His and hers chairs face the fireplace, along with a shared table in between with reading lamps for each.

Pattern in the textiles plays against the wood surround of timber frame and log walls. A black finish on the kitchen cabinetry adds antique appeal.

Trophies adorn the main gathering area of a spacious hunting cabin, where friends gather before the fire to share stories, or to take part in a competitive card game.

A loft takes a small bite out of the cathedral space that encapsulates a greatroom. Log walls caped by a second floor of barn-wood siding emphasize the natural palette of the surroundings.

Feminine flair in the furnishings adds delicacy to a cathedral space framed in logs.

Antiques and outdoors are thematic elements in this vacation retreat's greatroom.

A fieldstone fireplace warms a sitting area defined by a braided rug and an eclectic mix of inviting furniture.

A view through the massive beams that support this structure reveals the extent of the greatroom, where living, dining, and loft areas are all connected beneath a great cathedral ceiling.

A lofty overview encompasses the living area of a fire-lit greatroom.

Native American motifs in the textiles add color and ambiance to a rich, log room.

Wide plank flooring, the large over-sized fireplace and mighty beams overhead emphasize the scale of this greatroom.

Neutral furnishings allow the home's architecture to predominate in this impressive, soaring space.

Dark massive furnishings provide contrast with the rich wood surroundings to create a cozy atmosphere.

This gameroom is the ultimate living area for all who get to experience it, with a bar, wide screen TV, pool table, there is plenty to do.

An enormous living and dining area is located just inside the front entrance, an instant welcome to all guests.

In a modern twist on historic design, glass panels fill the spaces between post and beam on the gable wall of a log home. The effect is a brilliantly lit greatroom still sheltered by sturdy log walls as authentic as those enjoyed by our ancestors.

A log wall ascends two stories to the cathedral ceiling, the irregular profile of the logs and a varied finish creating a historic patina for the greatroom.

A stretch of staircase backs a greatroom, emphasizing the presence of the loft behind.

Character branches are used to create the balusters in this one-of-a-kind railing for an L-shaped staircase.

Kitchens

oday's kitchen has little in common with the log home kitchens of yesterday, from the modern appliances to the built-in cabinets and running water. Still, careful planning and a sense of nostalgia manage to unite the aesthetic with the practical, and kitchens in today's log homes still come off seemingly straight out of a simpler time and place.

A ladder interrupts this kitchen, ascending to a sparsely-furnished loft. The kitchen is furnished very much in the style of early homes, with the emphasis on the basics—fire, water, and a cupboard for the serving ware.

Contemporary appliances were designed to look antique, like this old-fashioned, footed range center. The unique countertop was crafted from concrete, with wrought-iron insets for the decorative trim.

Hickory cabinets give multi-toned dimension to the cabine-try, in keeping with the log home structure. A random tile mosaic backsplash creates an infusion of color.

White cabinetry create an area in contrast with the log surrounds, creating a culinary oasis.

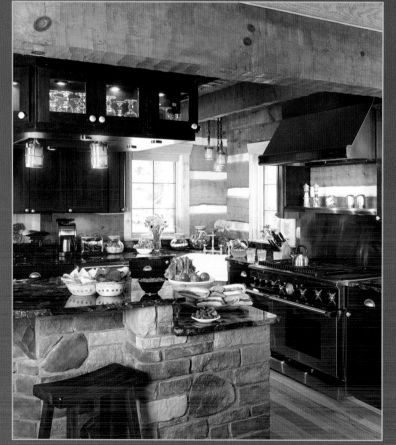

Black mutes the cabinetry and stainless-steel range within the wood environment. Stone forms an island for dining and food preparation.

Kitchen and dining areas
cohabitate a soaring space,
backed by a rugged log wall.

A range hood is cleverly disguised as a fireplace surround in this kitchen rich with historic character.

A fireplace evokes the cooking hearths of the past, although electricity and modern appliances happily serve this kitchen; the homeowner still uses the Dutch oven on various occasions.

Knotty pine
cabinetry
and eclectic
dinnerware lend
country charm

The homeowners
of this cabin opted
for a rounded edge
to be applied to the
hand-hewn floor
beams.

An antique olive finish characterizes the cabinetry in this kitchen, with a farmer's sink evoking grandma's habitat.

A cook looks out from a corner of the greatroom, the kitchen part of a larger living complex that makes sure she's never left out while busy fixing for everyone.

Heirloom-worthy furnishings outfit a kitchen, watched over by a beamed beadboard ceiling.

Tractor seats snug up to a countertop that flanks a kitchen under the loft. Contemporary stainless steel serves the cook, while wood surroundings keep her grounded.

Shaker-like furnishings affirm the simplicity of the surroundings and the owner's aesthetic vision.

A mix of old with the stainless steel of new are married for a contemporary kitchen firmly set in yesterday's style.

Alpine trees outline a central light as unique as the tile countertop it illuminates.

Glass-fronted cabinetry adds the illusion of windows to this kitchen nook, and white appliances create a visual pause.

A refrigerator of porcelain and chrome mimics materials and design of earlier days, as does a footed-island work station.

Dining Rooms

An essential amenity for those who entertain or host family gatherings, the dining room often occupies a key place in the home—a slice of a great view, and piece of real estate near kitchen and family room. Though it generally isn't used daily, it's certainly seen, so these rooms were thoughtfully planned and furnished to act effectively as showpieces. In this section, we explore both the casual spaces where family members dine daily, to the more impressive tables set for special company. In all cases, we chose projects that embody sensitivity to the log home lifestyle.

The dining experience in this cabin offers a plethora of focal points in viewing the multiple antiques that fill the space.

The Davy Crockett Tavern and Museum in Morristown, Tennessee, has been recreated to showcase how kitchens functioned in early American homes. The bench seats easily relocated to accomplish tasks, while cooking took place in the wide hearth.

A casual breakfast nook, furnished country style.

A bird's-eye-view encompasses a table and benches fashioned after the dining tables of our forefathers. Antiques and country-style furnishings complete the effect.

Tools and baskets hang at the ready on a log home, underlined by a dining set that emphasized the simple utility of this space. When not in use, the table can be raised to create more floor space.

A corner cupboard is considerably bigger than those utilized by the homeowner's ancestors, but the sense of style has changed little, right down to the gingham tablecloth.

Dovetail joinery makes a most welcome intrusion into this eating space, helping to define a bump-out breakfast nook. A braided rug and early American-style chairs emphasize a love of history, and the ease of living it.

Windsor chairs were stretched a tad to enable tavern dining at this home beverage center.

Straight-back chairs punctuate a long dining table amidst the stately walls of log and plaster.

A cathedral ceiling caps this impressive dining area, designed for high-power entertaining next to an old-fashioned fire.

A corner cabinet, mullioned windows, and a wealth of wood surround this cheerful breakfast nook.

Stately elegance in the appointments sit in quiet contrast to the random-profile logs that form the walls of this dining area.

Feminine touches highlight this wood-encompassed dining area, open to the outside via French doors.

A weathered gray finish adds patina to the stately dining room of a country home, where Windsor chairs encircle the dining table.

A dining nook was tucked neatly under a loft, with room to slide out should a crowd need accommodation.

A buffalo crowns a rise of fieldstone chimney overlooking this dining room.

The dining table commands a central position in this dog-trot style home, within eye and earshot of rooms on both the first and second floors.

A table set for six is flanked by benches, the ultimate in communal family dining experiences.

China cabinets and log form one side
of the dining area, glass another.

French doors make the inside feel like
out in this family dining nook.

A pretty picture window and a stone fireplace
compete for attention in a dining room.

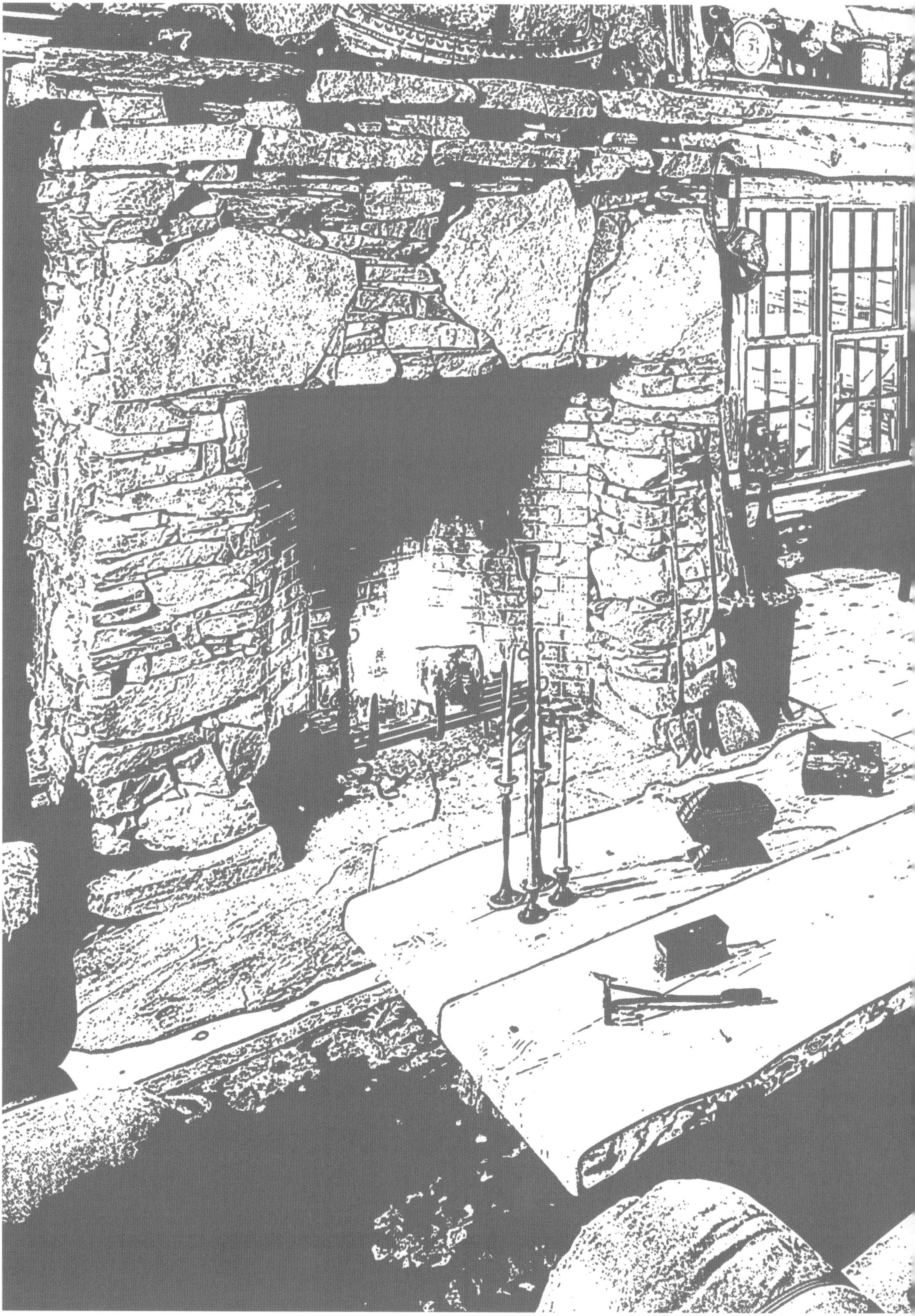

Fireplaces

"Heart" and "Hearth" are similar words for a reason. It is very hard to find a custom-built log home today that doesn't include an amazing fireplace as its centerpiece. This is a great opportunity to study style and design, as well as the all-important materials that go into creating that rustic hearth perfect for log home living.

This stone chimney contains a mock "keystone" in the center. The gas-powered fireplace is offset in the corner of a log home.

Fieldstone beautifies the surface of a stone fireplace surround, flanked by log walls and antique tools.

A flush chimney tapers at the loft level, emphasizing the adjustment in texture between log and stone.

An unusual stone arch caps this fireplace surround, set flush in a wood-paneled wall.

An assortment of sizes lend character to the stone surround of a rustic chimney setting.

A trophy fish is in keeping with the scale of an enormous stone chimney.

An assortment of small treasures populates the mantel piece, emphasizing the height of the stone chimney above. Further up, turtle art highlights the breadth of stone for admirers on the second floor.

Stone fills the gap between sun-filled windows by day, and warm hearth by night.

A fieldstone chimney rises through a second-floor loft, creating a warm central column for the entire home.

If you can't beat 'em, join 'em: A wide-screen television shares central billing with the stone fireplace and chimney.

A fieldstone fireplace recalls the humble hearths of early American homes.

The backdrop of slate frames an incredible mantel. A rock and ironwork were artfully embedded in a concrete mantel, attached to the wall and suspended by chains.

An artful brick mason crafted this handsome chimney, framed by a
unique custom designed, hand-hewn wood truss.

A central fireplace warms the entire home, rising through the center and forming a massive stone chamber to radiate warmth and beauty.

A broad mantel lends itself to seasonal decorating, working as the central showpiece in the home.

A stone chimney climbs in three stages through the cathedral ceiling of this greatroom. A potbellied, wood-burning stove ties into the chimney on one side to heat the home, while the hearth provides glow.

Wood caps a stone fireplace, in keeping with a room dedicated to forestry products.

Trophy deer flank a soaring chimney of stone.

Other Rooms

Being custom made, log homes often play host to a room designed with a specific owner purpose in mind. Here are some wonderful examples. Today's log cabins tend to be a little bigger than those of yore, and they contain some unexpected surprises.

A basement gameroom was finished in log veneer and non-structural decorative beams to tie it in with the rest of a log home.

A brick and stone hearth and log walls enclose a gentlemen's getaway room.

A billiards and bar share space in a wood-clad gameroom.

A simple log bump-out creates a sunny nook perfectly suited for two and tea.

A gunroom houses a favorite collection, buttressed by sturdy timber-frame and log siding.

A home office is packed with a lifetime
of mementoes and treasures.

There's not a washboard in sight: This log cabin extension is home to a home-maker's most modern conveniences. It's also a convenient mudroom for the entire family.

A home office is dedicated to the trees from which it came—the logs of the walls finished in their natural contoured profiles, and de-barked cypress tree trunks supporting the girder beam overhead.

Lofts

Once bedchambers to the youngest members of the family, lofts today are, well, more lofty! Often they overlook an expansive great room, and are large enough to serve as rooms unto themselves, or simply as antechambers to upstairs bedrooms. In an open floor plan, space under a cathedral ceiling is often set aside as a guest room, or a special nook where one can escape to read, to nap, or to play at some hobby or another. Here are a few examples of lofts, as seen from above and below.

A catwalk and loft area are accessed via a straight-shot staircase to the right of a dining area.

A sitting area serves as an intimate retreat for friends or to savor solitary moments.

A loft is magical, if for no other reason than the opportunity it offers to rise above it all. Besides being able to survey the greatroom and the view beyond the windows, a loft takes one up amidst the very timbers that support an open roof, where architecture becomes inspiration.

A fireplace warms a lofty sitting area, making this a favorite hangout spot.

Rustic furniture perfects an intimate retreat space.

Timber and reclaimed barn wood define this little loft space.

This stone chimney expands to create a lofty display shelf enroute on its rise through the roof.

A feminine touch characterized this spacious bonus room at the top of the home, with large, massive timber trusses.

A bedroom offers access to a little loft space, an invitation no child can resist.

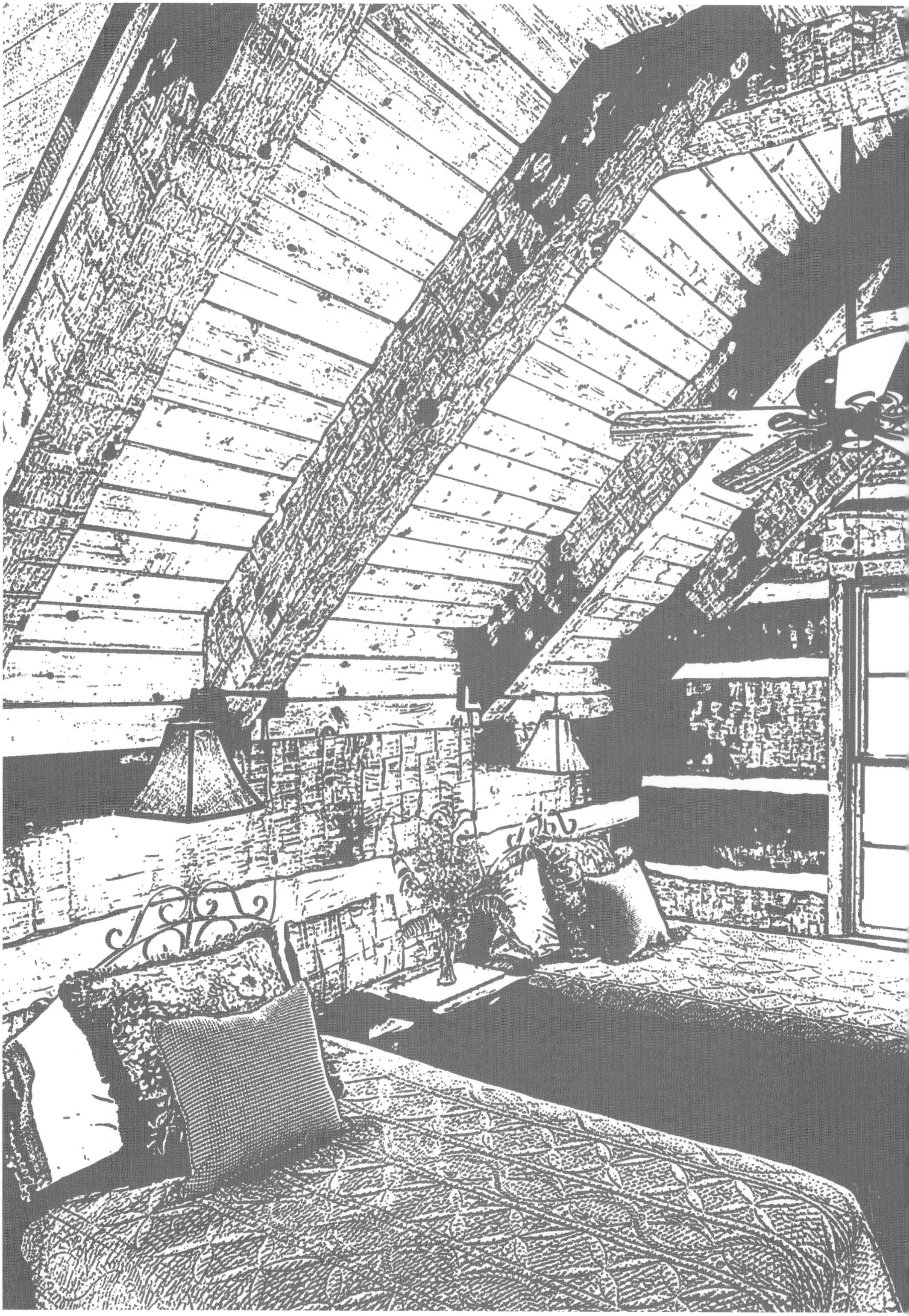

Bedrooms

The charm and coziness of a log home are best reflected in quilt-padded bedrooms and the sentimental décor that tends to find its way into the most intimate of rooms. The opportunities to decorate with log siding as a backdrop are endless. In this case, we've limited the options to those that seem appropriate to the historic context of log cabin living. There's also a section at the end devoted to the bunkroom—the nostalgic children's quarters of yesterday, as well as those fondly remembered from vacation retreats. Here is a fifty-cent tour of rooms not generally encountered by guests.

The Davy Crockett Tavern and Museum in Morristown, Tennessee, has been recreated and includes a bedroom furnished much as the pioneer's own quarters might have looked.

Rustic furniture is typical of the decor fashionable among log home owners. A skin rug and sporting memorabilia complete the hunting cabin look.

A trophy overlooks the decor in this eclectic master suite, where casual rules nothing out in a blending of different tastes.

Furnishings take a subtle back seat to the wood that was lovingly endowed on this master suite, from floor to ceiling.

Drywall finishes on interior walls introduce opportunities for color, and a perfect place for a display of furnishings or artwork.

The timbers of
a cathedral ceiling
are finished with a
weathered gray, as
are the log homes
in this muted,
relaxed suite.

Lots of color, from the textiles to the stones on the fireplace surround, add interest to this room.

The natural profile of the log walls creates a wonderful sense of timelessness for this guest room.

A feminine touch is in keeping with a log bedroom, especially one endowed with a big bank of windows.

A well-chosen quilt is all the decor a log room needs to set its own page in history.

Naturally contoured Bob Timberlake® logs with a hand-hewn finish make this room a wonder to contemplate from the comfort of a soft guest bed.

A lifetime of travel is distilled in a room of colorful treasures, all at home in this ancestral architecture.

The beadboard ceiling and knotty pine floor were set at opposing angles, adding a feeling of movement to the anchored log wall with fireplace.

Heavy timbers create a sheltered cave, with the outdoors easily accessed.

Character embodies this room with post crafted from whole tree trunks that create an outside feel for this cabin retreat.

A lofty bedroom is all the more majestic when furnished with a four-poster bed and a dramatic cathedral ceiling.

Pretty whites and blues
add country appeal in har-
mony with a natural finish
on log walls.

A rustic highboard bed is perfect in a log cabin home, made more feminine with the addition of floral textiles.

Primary colors in a quilt are the perfect complement to the natural finished log walls and whitewashed ceiling.

Twin beds are topped with thick blankets featuring a Native American motif.

A bear is right at home among the rustic furnishings of this bedroom den.

Painted plank walls are an appealing finish for the rustic interiors of a log cabin.

Pine board and batten is the perfect finish for a log cabin bunk room.

Flexible accommodations are critical in a weekend-retreat cabin.

Bunkbeds are the perfect furnishing for a loft in a weekend cabin
sporadically packed with friends and family.

Twins tucked under the eaves are always at the ready
for friends and family.

The architectural angles created by a dormer window add intrigue to a lofty guest bedroom.

Inviting guest beds command a lofty view, each illuminated by a window.

A lofty playroom is the perfect invitation for young family members to come and visit.

Baths

The early inhabitants of log homes went out to a smaller house for their constitutionals, and baths were an occasional occurrence in a tin tub. Today's homeowners have expanded expectations for their ablutions, and today's log cabins are designed to exceed them. Again, enjoy a tour of intimate spaces lovingly designed and furnished.

A glass shower is a great way to preserve the view of log siding.

A **sunken tub** brings the spa experience home in this log cabin master bath.

Pebble mosaic, a wooden tub, barrel sink, and a flagstone floor offer a stylish reinterpretation of the frontier bath.

Tile and wood team up to frame the best to be had in today's bathroom furnishings.

Built-in cabinetry in a natural wood finish is a nice accompaniment to an outside log wall, and a wonderful way to keep linens and other hygienic accouterments neatly organized and out of sight.

A claw-footed tub is right at home in a lofty master-suite bath.

A bay window view adds air to bubbles for a bath in this comfy footed tub.

Hickory cabinetry and pine paneling set at varying angles add intrigue to an architectural nook.

A skirted copper tub is right out of the Old West, and right at home
with log walls.

Pine paneling forms a nice marriage with an exterior log wall.

A skirted tub doubles as shower stall, the suspended curtain another wonderful relic of an era gone by.

A corner tub offers maximum bathing room while taking a minimum amount of space.

Bath furnishings are as true to history as one could hope for, while still promising a refreshing shower straight from a modern hot-water heater.

Built-in cabinetry and *his and hers* sinks perfect a master suite.

Wood logs are a wonderful backdrop for any furnishing or art.

A one-of-a-kind sink pedestal draws on nature for its form, while a toilet seat draws on history for its design.

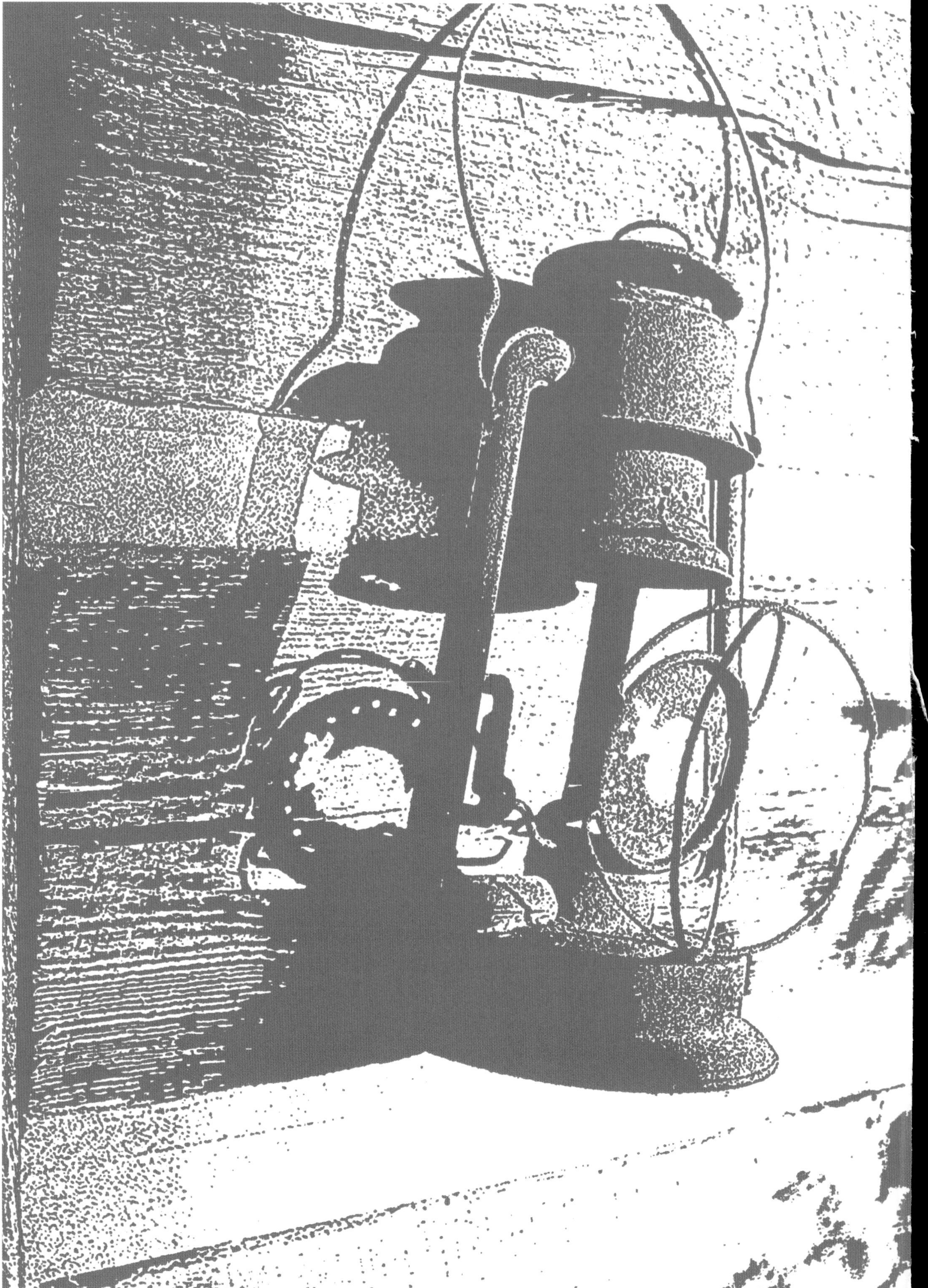

Lighting

Wonderful examples of exceptional lighting are featured throughout this book. We thought it would be worth focusing on a few examples, just to inspire and delight. Log cabin homes cry out for the unique and interesting.

This modern replica of a hand-held lantern provides interest, as well as a well-lit path.

This unique lighting piece continues the cabin theme with the backlit Alpine trees creating interesting shadows.